Designing Metrics

Crafting balanced measures

for managing performance

D0062803

by Dr. Bob Frost

Published by
Measurement International
P. O. Box 7848
Dallas, Texas 75209-0848

ISBN 978-0-9702471-2-4

Contents

3

Preface

In this book you will discover many key concepts about designing performance metrics for your enterprise or workgroup. The ideas it offers will better equip you to wrestle with the central question in balanced performance metrics: What to Measure?

This book, *Designing Metrics,* grew out of our projects advising and assisting organizations on metrics and business processes. In that work, we saw the need for a summary of the most straightforward, useful ways to think about and design measures for managing performance.

Designing Metrics was written to help your organization prepare for productive work on measuring performance. Organizations differ, so you will not find any one-size-fits-all answers to what you should measure. Experience has shown that the solution must be specific to your organization and your circumstances. As you select the concepts and tools here that best apply to your situation, you will be taking the first step toward the custom design you need.

Dr. Bob Frost

Part 1

Introduction

- The New Metrics

- Multiple Perspectives

- A Balancing Act

- Valuable Change

The New Metrics

"Today's management accounting information, driven by the procedures and cycle of the organization's financial reporting system, is too late, too aggregated, and too distorted to be relevant for managers' planning and control decisions."
—Johnson and Kaplan

If you have been looking into performance metrics, surely you have noticed how much things have changed in recent years. Not long ago, "performance measures" in business meant financial measures, plain and simple. In government and nonprofits, they meant "mission accomplishment." While such measures are still the bottom line for most organizations, they have been complemented by a wide range of new "balanced" measures that track the key factors behind financial or mission performance.

This change in metrics began back in 1987, when Johnson and Kaplan[1] published a book titled *Relevance Lost, the Rise and Fall of Management Accounting*. In it, the authors suggested that traditional accounting measures were too late and too distorted to be useful for directing organizational performance in the fast-paced, competitive business environment we face today. In short order, Kaplan and Norton[2] published a recommended solution—a performance model titled the Balanced Scorecard. Before long, a steady stream of books and papers came forth exploring performance measurement and suggesting how business performance could be better measured and managed.

By the 1990's, non-profit and government organizations were also vigorously exploring improved performance measures. A wide range of organizations began to see the needs: 1) to better understand performance; 2) measure how they are doing; 3) improve accountability; 4) and manage the processes that lead to performance. That trend continues today and further advances are being made in how the performance of organizations of all types can be better measured and managed. Approximately 80% of Fortune 500 companies say they use a version of balanced performance metrics and the same trend is clearly evident in nonprofits and government.

Where are we today? How can we summarize the changes taking place? Here is a chart to illustrate them:

Older Metrics	**Today's Metrics**
One perspective	Multiple perspectives
After the fact	Real-time tracking
Not actionable	Line of sight to action
Show snapshots	Show trends
Presented in tables	Presented graphically
Rob-Peter-Pay-Paul	Balance opposing forces

With the older metrics, business performance was generally measured from only the financial perspective.

These measures tended to be after the fact and not directly actionable by most employees. They showed a snapshot of performance at one point in time; they relied largely on tables for presentation; they readily allowed people to improve one aspect of performance (for example, short-term earnings) by sacrificing other aspects of performance (such as product research or customer service). Though performance metrics today still have a long way to go, the best ones are distinguished by an entirely new set of characteristics. The best metrics now show performance from multiple perspectives, giving a set of balanced indicators that reflect several aspects of how the organization is doing. They strive for real-time reporting that allows for performance adjustments before financial results are impacted. They attempt to give employees at all levels a direct line of sight so they can see how their actions can move the indicators in favorable directions. Finally, today's metrics are often presented as graphs that show a "movie" of performance trends over time rather than still snapshots of point-in-time performance.

> *"Proverbial wisdom counsels against risk and change. But sitting ducks fair worst of all."*
> –Mason Cooley

How far will this trend go? No one knows. A large majority of forward-looking organizations in every corner of the business, nonprofit and government worlds are finding powerful advantages in the new metrics and

8

using them to define and guide performance. Managers, leaders, and teams at all levels are using the new metrics to track performance, adjust actions, ensure accountability, and improve performance. High performance is the key demand placed on organizations today, and well designed metrics are the key tool in achieving it.

> *"A survey before the scorecard showed that 20 percent of employees understood the corporation's strategy; 80 percent understood it after the scorecard was put in place."*
>
> –William Halpern

Multiple Perspectives

"Think of business as a ball game. If you want to know who won the game, look at the scoreboard. But, if you are the losing team and want to win the next game, you can't get better by watching the scoreboard. You have to focus on improving your batting, pitching, fielding, and catching. . ."

–Gary Zeune

As we saw earlier, the biggest change in metrics in recent years has been the wide acceptance of the idea that financial metrics alone do not provide enough help in understanding and managing performance.

Similarly in sports, a team does not get better by watching the final score. In most organizations, the metrics equivalent to batting, pitching and fielding are things like *customer satisfaction, innovation, total delivered cost, on-time performance, process efficiency,* and so forth. Measures of these things tell the performance story in a richer, truer way than financial measures alone. They show how we must balance performance factors; they give variables to manage that we can get our hands on.

Multiple Perspectives. Let's illustrate the value of multiple perspectives with a simple exercise. Suppose an organization tracks performance from only the financial perspective. And, let's suppose its 3-year financial performance looks like the chart on the following page:

Earnings

2004   2005   2006

What does this chart tell us? What lies ahead? What action will we take? We can see that earnings are trending down, but we have no idea what factors are involved. Are we in a weak economy? Are costs growing too much? Is our industry in a downturn? Are we failing to keep up with competitors? Are we overstaffed? Truth is, all we have is a wakeup call; we know little about what is happening or what we should do about it. Without more information, our most likely course of action may be simple cost cutting.

Now, let's consider another scenario—one in which we measure performance from four perspectives:

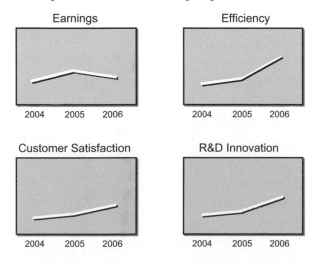

11

What may be happening in this case? What lies ahead? What might these multi-perspective metrics lead us to do?

While these multi-perspective charts may still leave us looking for final answers, we certainly have a great deal more to go on and we can, even with only four measures, generate some important hypotheses to check before taking action.

This exercise illustrates how balanced, multi-perspective metrics provide a richer, truer understanding of group performance. Here's another example. What do you see happening in this case?

People often say this group of charts represents an organization that is "milking the cow." That is, extracting the maximum from a dying business. And you can probably think of other interpretations that might apply.

Though we have been using only four measures in this exercise, you can pretty clearly see how additional perspectives give a more balanced picture of performance. Of course, with a full set of metrics designed to apply specifically to your organization or workgroup, the picture becomes much fuller and richer. This accounts, in part, for the popularity and usefulness of the new metrics.

A Balancing Act

*"Whatever has overstepped its due bounds is always in a
state of instability."* —Seneca

A balanced understanding of performance and balanced
actions in managing performance are two great goals of the
new metrics. Inside every organization, there are certain
forces, goals, or value systems that tend to oppose one
another. These include efforts to satisfy the customer, cut
costs, constantly improve processes, develop new products
and services for the future, return earnings to shareholders,
improve the stock price, improve workplace safety, maximize
market share, maintain the environment, and many others.
If any of these worthy goals becomes the sole guiding light of
the organization, many other legitimate goals will be
sacrificed—resulting in imbalanced efforts and, often, an
early demise for the organization.

Let's consider a simple example. Suppose we operate a
large, wholly-owned pizza chain. Our stores offer both
restaurant service and delivered pizzas. One day our Cost
Efficiency Department sends out a proposal saying, among
other things, "With our daily manufacturing volume of
2,000,000 pizzas, every cost must be carefully monitored. We
propose to put three fewer shreds of cheese on each pizza,
reducing our unit cost by 1 cent. Customers will not miss the
three shreds of cheese and, with our volume, this will put an

additional $20,000 daily on our bottom line, or about $7.2 million annually."

When the Marketing Department hears this proposal, they "go ballistic." In their view, this approach is completely wrongheaded. They send out a counter-proposal, one that begins with an old quote from the quality movement "You can continue taking small bits of cheese off the pizza . . . until there aren't any customers left!" Their counter-proposal goes on to say, "We propose the exact opposite. If we *add* two cents worth of cheese to each pizza, customers *will notice* and we project an expanded sales of 8%. Our unit cost will increase slightly, but the added revenue will improve earnings performance about $18 million annually."

So, how much cheese should be on the pizza? Should we follow the cost-cutting approach, the marketing approach, or leave things as they are?

A Balancing Act. Our pizza company is a graphic way to remember that opposing forces are always at work in every organization. How much of our cost savings should be passed on to customers to increase market share and how much should be returned to shareholders? How much shall we spend on new product research and how much on improved manufacturing processes? How much on advertising and how much on employee benefits? Shall we

15

move to better facilities or allocate more funds to serve clients? We have all been there. . . supporting actions that we believe will serve our organization better than some alternative course of action. It is the nature of organizational life. Though sometimes annoying, these controversies—these opposing forces—are a good thing, a healthy thing. If any particular force is allowed to run completely unchecked and unbalanced, even the one we wholeheartedly support, it will almost always lead to disaster for the organization. Whether it is cost cutting, customer service, or anything else. The goal of management, and the reason excellence in management is so difficult, is balanced achievement of multiple goals, not the optimization of one thing at the expense of all else.

Well developed, multi-perspective metrics cannot make management decisions for you. They cannot tell you how much cheese to put on the pizza. They cannot resolve the dilemmas presented by opposing forces. They can, however, help you paint a balanced picture of performance as the background for decision making. If we measure only the cost of things and never the value we derive, we will surely become zealous cost cutters. If we measure only our quality of service and never the cost to us or the benefit in retaining customers, we are sure to be threatened by the competitor who can better track our customers' price/quality preferences.

16

Valuable Change

"... they transformed an underperforming organization that was inwardly focused, bureaucratic, and inefficient into the leader in its industry--a turnaround that improved operating cash flow by more than $1 billion per year."   –Kaplan and Norton

Let's consider a real-world case. The case is Mobil Oil, one widely cited in the Balanced Scorecard literature. Mobil adopted the Balanced Scorecard approach to performance metrics relatively early, in 1994.

What was the result? Kaplan and Norton[3] report that early in 1995, shortly after Mobil started using the Balanced Scorecard, revenues and earnings suddenly fell well below budget. This was due to a relatively warm winter that reduced the sale of heating oil. When performance was reviewed at a top management meeting in April, managers saw a new culture begin to take shape. The CEO ackowledged the poor financial performance, but also noted the good performance reported on other scorecard factors, the "controllable" factors. On those factors, the story was good—expenses were down, market share was up, employee satisfaction was up. The CEO was quoted as saying "In all the areas we could control, we moved the needle in the right direction." The company had concluded that its new metrics showed that its strategy was being implemented and was succeeding—in spite of how external factors had weakened its financial performance. The company had succeeded in distinguishing between its long-term strategic success and its

17

short-term operational issues in a new way, allowing more focus to be placed on long-term success.

Furthermore, Mobil quickly went on to become one of the biggest turnaround stories in American business. The company moved from the bottom to the top of its peer group in profitability in a few short years by: 1) restructuring the organization; 2) introducing a new strategy; and 3) using a performance management process based on the new, balanced metrics. While the new metrics and scorecard cannot be given all the credit, they were a key management tool. A division executive was quoted as saying "The Scorecard gets the lion's share of the credit. We created a performance mind-set with the Balanced Scorecard."

And there is more to the story. Shortly after the turnaround, Mobil merged with Exxon to become Exxon Mobil, one of the world's largest companies. During the turnaround, Mobil had brought its Return on Capital up from 6% to 16%, cash flow up 200%, increased customer satisfaction, improved dealer quality and operations, reduced expenses 20%, and gone from last to first in profitability. When Mobil merged with Exxon, some analysts valued the merger at $60 billion, some at $80 billion, some at over $100 billion. No matter the exact figure, it is clear that the turnaround greatly increased Mobil's value in the merger and, at the end of the day, added billions of dollars of value for its shareholders.

This case is not unique. In our own practice, we have seen business organizations here and abroad follow similar paths. They have adopted new strategies, used new metrics based on those strategies to manage performance, and accomplished major turnarounds. In at least two cases, these businesses also merged with other organizations, as Mobil did, adding hundreds of millions, if not billions, of dollars in shareholder value through their improved performance.

> *"In a time of drastic change, it is the learners who inherit the future."* –Eric Hoffer

So, one of the most compelling advantages of the new metrics is that they help managers at all levels create stable employment and build stronger, more valuable organizations through better performance. Other advantages of the new metrics include their ability to bring a balanced picture of performance to management reviews, as we saw in the Mobil case. The new metrics are designed to make strategy specific and actionable, rather than merely a conceptual idea. For managers at all levels, the new metrics have proven a crucial tool that enables them to manage the factors that drive success.

In summary, properly-developed, balanced performance metrics offer:

- A balanced picture of performance

- The tools to convert strategy into action

- The means to manage factors that drive success

- A way to grow the value of the organization

We have relied primarily on one example here, and that from the world of business. There are many other cases, including many from the nonprofit and government sectors, that show how well-designed, balanced metrics can be central in establishing a performance-oriented culture.

Part 2

Measurement Frameworks

- Introduction

- Balanced Scorecard

- Strategy Maps

- Stakeholder Framework

- Program Logic Model

- Enterprise Performance Framework

- Cascading Framework

Introduction

"There's nothing quite so practical as a good theory."
–Kurt Lewin

"What should we be measuring?" This question has become a central theme since the new, balanced metrics were first introduced. Because every enterprise and every workgroup exists to fulfill a different mission, there is no valid, one-size-fits-all answer to this question. In this section, we will focus on the most useful tools for developing the right answer to this question for your enterprise or workgroup.

Your chief tool in designing metrics is a measurement framework. While such a framework, or performance model, cannot give you the exact variables to measure, it can tell you what types of variables to consider and where to look. Measurement frameworks guide our thinking about what performance means and about what leads to sustainable success; they help define the Critical Success Factors (CSF's) that lead directly to your measures. The Balanced Scorecard is the best known of these measurement frameworks, and there are several others that have proven highly useful.

Sustainable success? We know what leads to non-sustainable success, cost cutting and the elimination of everything that has to do with strategy and long term success—R&D, number of employees, new product design, customer service, process improvement, and so forth.

Some executives have built careers on "saving" moribund companies through these methods, and moving on before any long-term consequences of their actions plunge the companies back into crisis.

These short-term solutions are not our interest here. We want to know what leads to sustainable, long-term success for your organization. What Critical Success Factors should we manage and pay attention to? What issues must we balance? What should we measure? What is our best path to high performance over the long term? These are the questions addressed by the various metrics frameworks. In some cases, perhaps, it seems completely obvious what performance factors we must

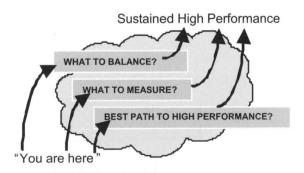

manage for sustained high performance. But usually it's not. And sometimes the obvious answers need to be checked by more rigorous thinking. Let's look at the most useful frameworks for doing that.

Balanced Scorecard

The Balanced Scorecard is a very popular measurement framework, and with good reason. This model has changed the way people approach performance metrics and had more influence on performance management in Fortune 500 companies than any other framework. And many organizations, like Mobil Oil, have credited the Balanced Scorecard as a key tool in changing their performance cultures and making significant performance gains. As the most popular metrics framework, use of the Balanced Scorecard has spread from the business world to government and nonprofit sectors.

Traditional Balanced Scorecard designs have four measurement perspectives—suggesting metrics should address performance in four categories: Financial, Internal Processes, Customers, and Learning & Growth.

THE BALANCED SCORECARD

When government and nonprofit organizations apply this framework, they often modify it by adding a perspective on Mission and placing less emphasis on the Financial perspective.

Financial Perspective. The measures that represent Financial performance answer the question "How do we look to owners/shareholders?" Examples might include earnings per share (EPS), stock price, return on assets (ROA), and other, more modern measures like Economic Value Added (EVA) for tracking and reporting the financial aspects of performance. Government and nonprofit organizations sometimes redefine this category as Mission success, refocusing it on measures of mission achievement and impact.

Internal Processes. The measures that represent Internal Processes answer the question "Are we improving how we operate?" They commonly track variables involving the quantity, quality, speed, cost, etc. of outputs and the processes by which the organization produces those outputs. A bank, for example, might track "speed of loan processing" or a manufacturing group might track "work in process" or "minutes of assembly time."

Customer Perspective. Measures in this category answer the question "How do we look to customers?" It is common for organizations to use customer satisfaction measures in this category and to augment them with leading indicators—other measures that have been shown to be tied to what customers value in the performance of the organization. In a bank or post office, for example, these might include line wait time, friendliness of service, etc.

Learning and Growth. Measures in this category address the question "Can we sustain our growth and position?" Measures in the Learning and Growth category are forward looking, concerned with how we are preparing for the future. Early Balanced Scorecards often used training time or training dollars as indicators here, but few have found such measures satisfactory. More success has been met with measures that show progress implementing change initiatives and new strategic directions. Measures in the Learning and Growth category are usually the most challenging measures to design, because they require organizations to think deeply about the future and about measuring the actions they truly believe will improve their strategic positions over time.

Strategy Maps

"Planning for change must be the ever-present concern of every single executive." –Jesse Werner

As we noted earlier, the Balanced Scorecard framework has proven extremely popular as a guide in designing new performance metrics in business and, to a growing degree, in government and nonprofit organizations. What is the logic behind the framework that has appealed to so many leading organizations?

From the beginning, the Balanced Scorecard has been tied to long-term thinking and strategy implementation. Indeed, one of the criticisms of traditional financial measures that led to the rise of balanced metrics is how they tend to ignore long-term issues and do not put adequate focus on implementing forward-looking strategies. To explain the strategic logic behind the Balanced Scorecard, Kaplan and Norton[3] published an adjunct to the Balanced Scorecard, a device called the "Strategy Map." A strategy map is specific to a given organization and shows how the strategy of the organization will be implemented through measureable actions and activities in each of the four performance perspectives.

Though the particular activities on a strategy map are specific to a given organization, strategy maps tend to have a common structure and logic. In each case, these maps show the "handles" by which people throughout the organization

27

can get a grip on the actions that will lead to strategic success. Most strategy maps follow a logic pattern similar to the one in this figure:

GENERIC STRATEGY MAP

Financial Perspective	Resulting in greater revenues, margins and profitability
Customer Perspective	Creating better results for customers and higher customer satisfaction
Internal Perspective	Which are necessary to create improved organizational processes and results
Learning/Growth Perspective	Strategic changes in organizational knowledge/understanding/capabilities

Commentary. The Balanced Scorecard framework, especially as augmented with a well-developed Strategy Map, has rightly enjoyed a great deal of success and popularity in designing metrics. Along the way, a few issues have also arisen in its use:

1) Fit. As they design metrics, some organizations and workgroups find that the Balanced Scorecard model does not fit their situations as well as they might like. Workgroups that are lower in the organizational structure, and particularly those where the work is highly operationally in nature, have not always found the Balanced Scorecard an easy fit. In some of these situations the highly strategic focus of this framework too far outweighs the operational aspects of their performance mix. When this framework is applied in such settings, it often happens that critical day-to-day operational factors are included as "strategic" and the term "strategic" becomes a watered-down synonym for "important" rather than retaining its full meaning.

2) Completeness. In designing metrics, some organizations have found the Balanced Scorecard does not include certain perspectives on performance that they consider vital. For example, some organizations consider an "Employee" or "People" perspective essential to their strategic model and have added it as a new category in their modified Balanced Scorecards.

Stakeholder Framework

"One thing is crucial to success in service, finding out who your customers are and what they expect." –O. Bjelland

Another model useful for designing metrics is the Stakeholder Framework. This simple, powerful framework came out of the Quality Movement of the past two decades. This framework is based on the idea that organizations serve and otherwise impact various groups of stakeholders, and how well they meet the expectations and requirements of these stakeholders is, by definition, a guide to measuring their performance. Those that provide their stakeholders (customers, owners, employees, suppliers, regulators, etc.) with what they want and expect better than others are the stronger performers. The use of this framework in designing metrics can be illustrated as follows:

THE STAKEHOLDER FRAMEWORK

Who are they?	What do they care about?	How can we measure it?

Owners, Customers, Employees,
Partners, Regulators . . .

In practice, applying this framework is straightforward and relatively easy. We identify who our stakeholders are—

customers, owners, employees, suppliers, regulators and others who have a vested interest in how we perform. Next we examine each group and carefully research what that group values or cares about in our performance. For example, in the business world, investors will care about things like stock price, dividends, and total return on investment. On the other hand, in a large nonprofit organization the funders may care about number of clients served, success rates, responsiveness, cost-efficiency, and so forth.

Each stakeholder group will have a different set of "careabouts" that lead to different performance metrics. In this way, the different stakeholder groups function somewhat like the four categories of measures in the Balanced Scorecard—they are different perspectives from which we view, track and evaluate performance. Overall, the most salient stakeholder "careabouts" become the performance factors we seek to measure.

Applying the Stakeholder Framework often reveals how key performance factors relate to one another. Sometimes, certain stakeholder interests will be aligned and support one another. More commonly, this framework reveals conflicting interests and shows how certain performance factors are in tension with one another and must be carefully balanced.

The Stakeholder Framework has several advantages in designing metrics. First, it applies readily to all organizational levels; whether we are considering a business unit, a functional area, a department or workgroup, people can easily identify who their stakeholders are. From there, it may involve some research and digging to determine the true stakeholder "careabouts." Sometimes the "careabouts" will be well known, but take note: following these assumptions without careful checking is dangerous.

Another advantage of this framework is how it gives a concrete, tangible way to think about the meaning of performance and how to define valid metrics. No abstract concepts here; we are considering real stakeholders and what those stakeholders require of us. Because of this, the Stakeholder Framework makes strong intuitive sense to people—when they hear it, they have a certain gut-level sense that this must be a correct and valid approach to thinking about performance. This is sometimes called "face validity"—the framework is valid just on the face of it.

A final advantage of the Stakeholder Framework is the useful balance and counterpoint it provides to heavily strategy-based frameworks like the Balanced Scorecard. The focus on stakeholders firmly grounds the Stakeholder Framework in the here-and-now—in other words, the day-to-day operational performance of the enterprise.

Commentary. While the operational emphasis of the Stakeholder Framework can bring a useful balance to strategy-based frameworks like the Balanced Scorecard, this is also its primary limitation. Used by itself, it will lead toward metrics for pleasing stakeholders in the here-and-now—providing them more of the same kind of performance they have historically valued.

This pressure toward the here-and-now can leave us blind to the need to make strategic changes—to alter the nature and basis of competition, to establish new and innovative approaches, to alter position in the marketplace, to create new types of products, etc. All these strategic issues tend to call for long-term actions that are not necessarily priorities for today's stakeholders and which may even run counter to their short-term interests. For example, many shareholders of pharmaceutical or software companies might prefer that profits be returned to them as dividends rather than invested in new product research.

All in all, the Stakeholder Framework is extremely useful in designing metrics, but must be accompanied by some means to ensure that long-term strategic issues are also represented in the metrics.

Program Logic Model

The Program Logic Model is a framework that captures and succinctly illustrates the big picture view of an entire organization, program or effort. This framework has enjoyed great popularity in government and nonprofit circles, yet remains relatively unknown in the business world.

The ideas behind the Program Logic Model have been around since the early 1970's. Over the years, various versions of the framework, and various enhancements, have been offered. In its simplest form, the way we will illustrate it here, the Program Logic Model describes the Inputs, Activities, Outputs and Outcomes of a program or organization.

We have all seen how government and nonprofit organizations have been increasingly required to demonstrate the success of their programs and become more accountable. In many cases, the Program Logic Model has helped such organizations develop powerful and succinct descriptions of their work and make great strides in performance management and accountability. By including stakeholder groups as they develop and review their logic models, these same organizations have been able to ensure that their programs respond to the real concerns of their stakeholders; they have been able to tie their activities and use of resources to their results in a way that generates both continued support and appropriate accountability.

In the past, demonstrating good accountability and the productive use of funds have been elusive goals for many nonprofit organizations. To see how the Program Logic Model can make the work of such agencies specific and concrete, let's consider a simple logic model from a hypothetical nonprofit called the Children's Choral Society.

Logic Model—Children's Choral Society

Inputs	Activities	Outputs	Outcomes
Resources:	Programs &	Learning:	Condition:
Human	Services:	--Musical literacy	--Changed lives
--Staff: (#)	--Choruses (#)	--Voice technique	--Musical careers
Financial	--Rehearsals (#)	--Discipline	--Civic mindedness
--Tuition ($)	--Performances (#)	--Diversity	--Community image
--Performances ($)	--Regional Tours	--Quality music	
--Contributions ($)	--National Tours	Community:	Measures:
Facilities	--School Concerts	--Support for music	
--Performance hall	--Summer Camp	--Chorale enrollment	
--Rehearsal space		--Patron attendance	
--Office space	Measures:	--City ambassadors	
Technologies			
--Ticketing system		Measures:	
--Attendance tracking			
--Donor database			
--Music library			
Measures:			

This figure shows how, on one page, a logic model can paint a picture of how an entire organization or program operates, how its *inputs and resources* flow to its *activities* which then lead to *outputs* or short-term results. These outputs, in turn, bring forth the broad, long-range *outcomes* that are the ultimate goals of the organization or program. When these four elements of a program—*resources, activities, outputs* 35 and *outcomes*—are carefully described, they form valid starting points for designing performance metrics. Even in this simplified example, you can see how the variables in the *activities* column could lead to measures for the Children's Choral Society. More importantly, you can see how the variables in the *outputs* and *outcomes* columns could be used, with a little creativity, as starting points for designing metrics—two categories of metrics that have been elusive, and in great demand, for organizations dedicated to the public good.

Commentary. The Program Logic Model makes explicit the logical linkage between program elements, much the same way a Strategy Map does for a Balanced Scorecard Framework. Many have used the Program Logic Model successfully in designing metrics, finding it lends itself well to both strategic and operational objectives. Though this framework has enjoyed clear success in governmental and nonprofit organizations, it is relatively untried in the business world. This framework is strongest when applied to individual programs or organizations with very targeted missions; it may require more effort at levels where complex agencies, institutions, or multi-program efforts are being measured.

Enterprise Performance Framework

"There is no resting place for an enterprise in a competitive economy." —Alfred P. Sloan

This framework for designing metrics pays particular attention to the competitive and economic pressures behind performance in today's economy. It is based on three fundamental ideas, all rooted in basic economics and the practical facts of life in a competitive economy:

1) Effectiveness. First is the idea that all organizations, from the United Nations down to a two-person department, have one thing in common—each is a collection of people who have come together for a common purpose. How well they fulfill that common purpose, that mission, therefore becomes one foundation for measuring their collective performance. In this framework, effectiveness—*how well the mission or common purpose is being fulfilled*—is one essential theme in any organization's metrics. When measures of effectiveness fall to a low level, the organization is no longer fulfilling its purpose. Such an organization is either 1) rapidly failing; 2) fulfilling some other valid purpose; or 3) being temporarily propped up by artificial means.

2) Efficiency. Secondly, we have the reality of competition and the accompanying need for efficiency.

37

Every organization, and every department within every organization, has competitors. There are always others who vie to fulfill the same mission, serve the same customers, or consume the same resources as we do. For a given level of quality and service, the most efficient provider always has a cost advantage that can be exploited; the cost advantage can be used to offer greater returns to shareholders, better prices to customers leading to increased sales and market share, etc. The less efficient providers are always at a disadvantage and under threat. These rules apply to business, nonprofit, and government organizations alike. Efficient nonprofits can accomplish the same mission

> *"In business, the competition will bite you if you keep running; if you stand still, they will swallow you."*
> –William S. Knudson

at less cost for their funders, fostering growth. Efficient government agencies can often add new missions or more easily get funded. The bottom line is that efficient organizations and departments—*those that consume the fewest resources to provide a certain benefit*—can use their efficiency to grow and prosper at the expense of others. In today's competitive world, efficiency in fulfilling a mission is a fundamental factor in measuring performance.

3) Strategic Improvement. Thirdly, we have the fact that all organizations today operate in a changing world, under changing circumstances, and with a constant need to improve their strategic positions for the future. In short, they must adapt, change, and constantly seek out better ways to compete, better ways to conduct operations, and better ways to benefit customers and stakeholders if they are to prosper over the long haul. Other organizations are aggressively pursuing such innovations and those that stand still in this race will soon be left behind. So success in creating strategic change is the third essential foundation for measuring performance.

The Framework. These three observations have resulted in a simple framework for measuring and managing

ENTERPRISE PERFORMANCE FRAMEWORK

performance called the Enterprise Performance Framework. This framework suggests that every type of organization, and every workgroup within a given organization, should consider three categories in designing performance metrics: *effectiveness, efficiency,* and *strategic improvement.* Every organization should consider measures of *effectiveness* that answer the question "How well are we fulfilling our mission?" Such measures are likely to include metrics on customer satisfaction, timeliness, quality, etc. Secondly, every organization should consider measures of *efficiency* that answer the questions "How efficiently are we operating in fulfilling our mission?" Or "How much is it costing us to produce a given output?" These measures may involve cost per unit, time per unit, % G&A expense, and so forth.

> *"If, in today's environment, you are not paranoid about competitors, you simply do not understand your situation."*
> –Gary Kaufman

Finally the Enterprise Performance Framework suggests that organizations look to measures of *strategic improvement* that answer the question "How well are we preparing for success tomorrow?" Metrics in this category may involve milestones toward accomplishing key strategic initiatives, progress in changing the basis of competition, progress in offering a new value proposition to customers, progress toward new organizational capabilities, etc.

So, the Enterprise Performance Framework suggests that, in designing metrics, every organization, and every department, should seek to track its *effectiveness*, its *efficiency*, and its *strategic improvement* for the future—a useful, general framework for understanding and measuring performance.

Cascading Framework

"Always look upward. To what higher-level goals must your group contribute?" —Lee Duff

The Cascading Framework is another important framework for designing metrics in any type of organization. This framework recognizes and uses the inherent structure of your organization. At the top, every organization has a mission and set of objectives or goals. To carry out these missions and objectives, organizations develop a structure of subunits or sub-organizations, each specializing in some type of work that helps the larger organization meet its goals. Or so the theory goes. . . For example, a typical business unit will have a number of functional areas and operating units under its umbrella, such as Finance, Human Resources, Legal, Manufacturing, Marketing, etc. These functional areas, in turn, have their own structure of departments. The Legal function might have departments for Patents, Contracts, Litigation, Risk Management and others. Human Resources might have departments for Recruiting, Employment, Benefits, Compensation and so forth. While these examples come from the business world, government and nonprofit organizations likewise have similar structures of sub-organizations to carry out their missions.

Over time, there is a tendency among sub-units of large organizations to take on lives of their own, to become partially autonomous. While they serve the larger organization, they also promote the best practices of the professions represented in their various departments. In short, they take on agendas of their own which are, in principle, supposed to serve the larger good of the enterprise. Sometimes their autonomy works for the good of the enterprise; sometimes it causes friction and wasted energy. It's a matter of balance.

In designing metrics, the Cascading Framework helps ensure alignment of effort within an organization, that all efforts add up to achieving the larger goals of the

CASCADING FRAMEWORK

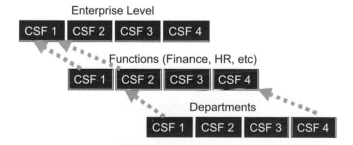

enterprise. To use this framework, each sub-unit in an organization must look to the goals and Critical Success Factors (CSF's) of the next higher level and ask "which of these goals and CSF's relate to our work, and what is our

43

role in achieving them?" By using this framework in designing metrics, an organization can ensure that its measures support an environment of strong accountability.

Let's consider an example. Suppose a high-tech business has determined that nanotechnology will be critical to its future success. The organization already has some capability in this field, but nowhere near what it will need, so increasing nanotechnology capability in the next three years has been set as a key strategic objective. As each major functional group in the business looks toward its own strategic objectives and performance metrics, it must ask whether it has a role in achieving this business objective and what that role is. Those in charge of Facilities may, in consulting with line management, realize that nanotechnology will require new and different workspace and equipment at a specific point in time. The R&D Library may realize that new books and subscriptions are in order. Human Resources may realize that new high caliber staff members must be onboard at a certain point in time, and so forth. These requirements become critical success factors for the various major functional areas in the business and help define their performance measures for the coming time periods.

Furthermore, as the various departments within Facilities, the R&D Library, and HR set their strategic objectives, they must likewise look to see what part of these next-higher-level objectives they must fulfill. For example, the Recruiting Department within HR may realize that it must, in a timely way, be prepared to support significant new recruiting efforts. This may call for additional consulting with R&D managers, learning where and how nanotech researchers are being recruited today, and integrating the required new efforts with other recruiting plans. These new requirements will be Critical Success Factors for Recruiting and will suggest specific performance metrics and performance tracking.

One of the benefits promised by modern, balanced performance measures is "alignment of effort." That is, getting everyone to pull in the same direction. You can readily see how the Cascading Framework helps ensure that efforts are aligned and measures of performance at each level establish a framework of accountability. Cascaded measures also provide leading indicators on whether strategic objectives will be met. If the measures established by Facilities or Recruiting suggest their objectives may not be met, then Operations or HR will know their objectives may be in jeopardy and the ultimate strategic objective of the business may likewise be in jeopardy. This framework for metrics, then,   45 provides a rationale for aligned efforts, much like the Strategy Map does in Balanced Scorecard designs. Proper reporting and monitoring of measures provides leading indicators by which management can proactively assure that strategic objectives will be achieved. This alignment of effort, and the establishment of effective leading indicators on key performance targets, are two of the benefits promised by the new metrics. Realizing these benefits is, in turn, one of the primary advantages of using the Cascading Framework.

Commentary. The usefulness of the Cascading Framework and its value in aligning effort across an organization are clear. Fully realizing these benefits calls for an extensive, top-down installation process. In other cases, such as when an isolated department or workgroup seeks to independently improve its performance, this framework may be less useful.

Part 3

Using the Frameworks

- Which Framework?

- Critical Success Factors

- Translating to Measures

- How Many Measures?

Which Framework?

"When you win, nothing hurts."   –Joe Namath

Measurement frameworks serve two important roles in managing performance.

1) First, they serve as guides in thinking about what performance actually means in your situation and in choosing the best set of measures to track performance.

2) Second, measurement frameworks serve a crucial communication purpose. They tie your metrics together in a package so that your performance reports tell a coherent story. They help you tell the story of performance so the reader can make sense of your metrics and your performance.

Right now, we are dealing with frameworks as they fulfill the first purpose—choosing the best set of metrics. The frameworks we have just reviewed are those that have proven the most useful and reliable guides in designing metrics. But, with all these frameworks to choose from, your organization may question "Which framework is best?"

Beware. There is not a simple answer to this question. In asking this question we are like the person who is making a major life decision—a person with four close friends, each of whom is respected for his or her wisdom, insight and concern. Would our hypothetical person consult just one of these friends in making this crucial decision? Probably not; a prudent person would likely consult all four, even though each friend may see the matter from a different perspective and offer a different way of thinking about it. Likewise with measurement frameworks. Though one framework may be our primary guide in a given design situation, we believe in learning from all of them.

As you know, the Balanced Scorecard framework has been very popular and successful, generating a valuable base of experience and many knowledge-sharing opportunities between organizations. At the same time, the Stakeholder Framework continues to bring a gut-level "correctness" that has wide appeal. And each of the other frameworks has its own appeal and value.

From our experience with businesses, nonprofits and government groups, we like this approach:

1) First, educate your organization on the key frameworks, exploring their advantages and disadvantages.

2) Second, choose a starting framework that somehow fits the circumstances best or is favored by the organization.

3) Third, after using the starting framework to generate a set of Critical Success Factors and measures, reconsider the other

frameworks to find any success factors that may have been overlooked. This method maintains a useful focus throughout the task, yet ensures that no critical factors are missed.

Remember, your goal is to determine your best list of Critical Success Factors and measures; the frameworks are merely different pathways for thinking about performance and getting the list of factors that will lead to sustained success.

Critical Success Factors

We've been using the term "Critical Success Factors" (CSF's) and you will often see this term in metrics work. The name says it all. Critical Success Factors are the "make or break" issues in the performance of your organization, enterprise or workgroup. They are the "must do" factors that determine whether you are successful today and whether you will succeed in the future. You probably know what some of these CSF's are for your organization.

We introduce CSF's at this point because we are transitioning from the *ideas* behind the measurement frameworks to the actual *work* of designing the metrics you need. As we noted earlier, one purpose of measurement frameworks is to guide thinking as we identify, define and agree on measures. Frameworks help in this task by suggesting or reminding us of factors that may be critical to success for our group—CSF's. While you sometimes can go directly from a category in a measurement framework (like "Customer") to the measures of how you are doing in that category, often you will use CSF's as an intermediate step. What is it about customers that is critical to our success? Do we need more of them; must they see us as better quality than our competitors; must they perceive our service or value differently than they now do? In short, what factors are critical to our success in the customer category? Those are the CSF's that help you design metrics.

51

With this realization, we can appreciate the various performance frameworks in a new light. It is not so much that one is correct and all the others incorrect in our application. Or that we must choose which is the most correct of the lot. Several measurement frameworks may seem "correct" and help illuminate our thinking about performance. Each framework may help us see CSF's that could have been missed if we had concentrated only on those suggested by some other framework—no matter how fitting or appropriate that framework seemed.

In actually designing measures, then, limiting ourselves to one way of thinking can be, well . . . limiting. Measurement frameworks, just like our mission, strategy, stakeholders and other factors, should be considered "thought tools" that help identify and clarify the Critical Success Factors in our situation. Even a perfectly strong and useful framework like the Balanced Scorecard can, if adopted too fervently and without broader thought, keep us from seeing other CSF's and strategic issues.

To illustrate this use of measurement frameworks in the design process, consider the Funnel Diagram. It shows how a wide variety of frameworks and input materials are all available to us as we begin the metrics design process. We are perfectly free and, in fact, encouraged to put all these items in our funnel of Thought Tools. Among them we may have a

FUNNEL DIAGRAM

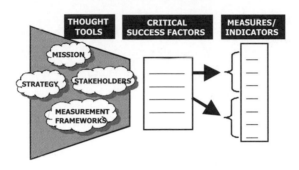

favorite or two, and perhaps some fit better than others. That's fine. But let us keep our minds open to the contributions of other Thought Tools as we explore what our final list of Critical Success Factors must contain. Sub-par results in the design of metrics often comes from the blind, rote application of some popular model, without diligent thought and consideration of the alternatives.

Translating to Measures

"An orderly method is the surest road to an orderly result."
–C. R. Snyder

Having applied the most suitable frameworks to better conceptualize performance and craft a list of Critical Success Factors, your next design task is translating the CSF's into measures and indicators.

This phase of designing metrics, as with the previous phase, calls for discussion, exploration and a good amount of give and take in your design group. Fortunately, there is at least one model to help guide this effort and keep things on track. Though now several years old, this model remains the most useful guide in this creative stage of designing metrics. The model, called the Three-step Method, was first introduced in our earlier book, *Measuring Performance* (ISBN 0-9702471-1-7).

"No man ever yet became great by imitation."
–Samuel Johnson

This process is called the Three-Step Method because defining performance indicators—deciding exactly what to measure—typically involves three distinct steps. In three steps, you translate a general performance topic into specific performance indicators.

Here's an example. In Step 1, your business strategy and measurement framework(s) help you list a set of perspectives or performance topics (e.g., financial, misson effectiveness, process efficiency, customer service, etc.). In Step 2, you determine where and how you must succeed on each topic, a set of Critical Success Factors. Earlier we noted how helpful measurement frameworks can be in determining the

THREE-STEP METHOD

STEP 1 →	STEP 2 →	STEP 3
Performance Topics	Critical Success Factors	Performance Indicators
Financial Performance		
.		
Market Performance		Phone Wait Time
.		
.	Quick Access ———	# Rings to Answer
.		
Customer Service ———	Accurate Info	Wait Time in Store Line
.		
.	Friendly Tone	
Product Development		

right performance topics and CSF's. For customer service, you might determine that these CSF's include quick access, accurate information, and friendly tone of service. In Step 3, you consider each Critical Success Factor (e.g. quick access) and define specific performance measures or indicators to track success. For your "quick access" factor, these might include *Telephone Wait Time, Number of Rings to Answer,* and *Wait Time in Line.*

The Three-Step Method is both important and useful in developing proper metrics, so you may want to take a minute to think through one or two examples on your own. You might try something like "new product research" or "manufacturing efficiency" or "improved market share" as performance topics.

> *"With method and logic one can accomplish anything."*
> –Agatha Christie

You can see that the three-step process works from the general to the specific—from a performance topic to Critical Success Factors to specific performance indicators. As we noted earlier, it is important to determine all the Critical Success Factors that apply to a given performance topic; any that are overlooked may be neglected in the management process, leading to a lack of balance and a distorted emphasis on some aspects of performance.

How Many Measures?

"When you arbitrarily reduce complexity to simplicity, you depart from reality." —Pete Sorenson

Everyone wants the right number of metrics. Some authorities even recommend fixed limits—10 to 15 measures, never more than eight, etc.

The reason, of course, is that you do not want to overwhelm your organization with too many measures. You want to measure and manage the "critical few" things that will really make a difference.

But there are three deadly arguments against arbitrarily limiting the number of metrics:

1) First, there are many important things you must monitor, even if they are not likely to change.

2) Second, there is complexity. Modern organizations are large and complex. You need a comprehensive picture of performance to guide understanding and decisions. Managing with a keyhole view can lead to disaster.

Ever look into the cockpit as you are boarding a flight? You probably saw that the pilot and copilot face a hundred or more dials and gauges. Would you want to limit them to 8-15?

Actually, only a few gauges are important to a pilot at any one time. The airspeed indicator is not important while the plane sits at the gate, for example. And only a few gauges are critical during takeoff or landing. And only a few at cruising altitude. But they're not the same few! The critical few change with conditions, so the pilot needs, in total, a full complement of gauges.

And it is the same with performance metrics in a large organization. Not all of your metrics will demand focused attention all the time, but if a few key ones are missing, your organization could be heading for a nosedive without realizing it.

3)   Third, there is the rob-Peter-to-pay-Paul problem. Anything not measured is subject to being sacrificed for the things that are measured. For some time it has been said, "What gets measured, gets done." Here we have the other side of that same coin, the one that says, "What doesn't get measured, might not get done." And some of what might not get done can be very important. From a management perspective, this is a powerful argument for comprehensive, well-thought-out metrics.

This is another version of the point we noted earlier; excellence in management is difficult is because it is about the balanced achievement of multiple goals, not the optimization of one thing at the expense of all else.

Your challenge in establishing performance metrics is to ensure that every Critical Success Factor at your level of the organization is represented and monitored, *and* that the critical few measures occupy center stage.

Is there any help? Yes. You might consider the designs of others who have solved, or partly solved, this problem. Some of the more common solutions involve: 1) foreground and background metrics; 2) tiers of metrics available by drill-down links; and 3) designs that distinguish between strategic metrics and monitored metrics. Excellent, specialized software packages are available for managing a large number of metrics while keeping the focus on a critical few.

Part 4

Staying on Track

- Signs of Success
- Signs of Trouble

Signs of Success

Several signs or indicators can help tell when you are on the right track with your metrics. Here are some of the best:

1) Relevant and crucial to success. If your indicators are carefully developed from your Critical Success Factors, they are very likely to excel as relevant and critical to success. Each measure should have a "pedigree" that logically links it directly back to what is necessary for your group or organization to succeed.

2) Actionable to users, line of sight. The best measures are actionable; users have a direct line of sight between their actions and the measures of success. In other words, they are useable on a regular daily basis.

3) Proper comparative(s). In measuring performance, one quickly discovers that good measures, by themselves, do not tell how you are doing. You need benchmarks or comparatives that are strategically and operationally relevant. Your own past performance is one good anchor, but it will not assure you of rising above the competition. You will need benchmarks or other ways of telling how well your performance stacks up against what it could be or should be.

4) Encourages right actions. When you measure performance and publicize the results, it affects behavior.

That's the whole idea. Do the measures you are proposing encourage the right kinds of behaviors and right kinds of decisions in your group or organization? Or do they encourage results you do not want?

5) Technically correct. Proper measures will be valid (measuring what you intend them to measure) and reliable (not influenced by random factors). They will make proper use of statistical procedures (not averaging percentages, proper sampling, measurement frequencies that match the change rates of variables being tracked, and so forth).

6) Clear, graphic reporting. The best performance measures are clear and often make use of graphical reporting methods to better communicate results. The worst performance reports are those with page after page of numerical tables printed in small type; a few simple line charts communicate better by illustrating trends and helping readers grasp conclusions visually.

7) Cost effective. While performance measures are important and valuable, their cost cannot exceed their worth if they are to be practical management tools.

These are all signs that you are on a good course with your metrics. We sometimes cannot have every desireable quality in our metrics, but must settle for a good balance. For example, sometimes we must sacrifice precision to include measures that we know are crucial. To paraphrase an old Peter Drucker saying, "Measuring the right things is more important than measuring things right"—in other words, a good estimate of a crucial variable is more important than four-decimal-point precision on something trivial.

Signs of Trouble

Just as it is useful to consider the signs we are on track in designing and using metrics, it can also be useful to consider the signs we may not be on the right track, or that our train has jumped the track altogether. There are many signs that we may be making a mistake or getting into trouble with metrics. Here are some to watch for:

1) Searching for perfection. One of the most significant temptations in designing metrics is to search for the perfect first design. Those who do so often end up in "analysis paralysis" and may not finish. We are not condoning hasty or thoughtless designs, but a good rule of thumb is that first designs in this work never are perfect—even when we think they are. First designs are nearly always adjusted or modified within a year as experience accumulates. The best

CONTINUOUS IMPROVEMENT MODEL

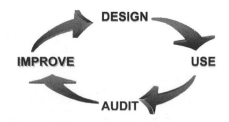

approach is to strive for a very good design, a 90% solution, and implement it; then apply periodic reviews and continuous improvement.

2) Seeking a one-number performance index. This is a controversial matter, as many people find the idea of a performance index compelling. We believe it is a red herring that you definitely should not chase. Our ultimate purpose in designing metrics is to better understand, report and manage performance. An index works directly against this goal by obscuring individual measures and allowing gains on one performance factor to mask lossses on another factor.

Furthermore, designing an index requires carefully assigning weights to each indicator in the index. Establishing valid weights usually requires great effort and endless discussions that are never repaid in usefulness.

"It's a little like the tale of the roadside merchant who was asked how he could sell rabbit sandwiches so cheaply. 'Well,' he said 'I have to put in some horse meat too. But I mix 'em fifty-fifty: one horse, one rabbit.'"
–D. Huff

The index is a compelling idea, but generally a mistake if our goal is to understand and manage performance.

3) Seeing unintended consequences. Another sure sign that we are on the wrong track with metrics is unintended consequences. For example, if our measures of efficiency are driving behaviors that bring unacceptable results in customer service, we obviously have a problem. And vice versa. Measuring two things, in this case efficiency and service, shows where the balance lies and we must determine if we are producing the results we want or whether we have misplaced the balance point. For another simple example, consider the case of the receptionist who constantly juggles 4 or 5 calls on hold because we measure whether each call is answered on the first ring; we have to ask whether we are creating what was intended.

4) Accepting vendor metrics unquestioned. Especially in outsourcing situations, it can be tempting to accept vendor-provided metrics as an easy solution for monitoring performance. Easy, but risky. We must always remember several key points about the metrics offered by vendors— they will be the metrics that are easiest and cheapest to collect; they will generally make the vendor's performance look good; and, most importantly, they will be metrics that were designed without *your* strategies, *your* goals and *your* priorities in mind. Metrics should always be based on *what you value* in vendor performance.

5) Looking under the lamp post. It happens every time. As a group works out their metrics design, someone will say "First, let's see what we have data on." While it is completely commendable to use existing data, we must always *begin* our quest by asking "What do we need to know to drive the performance of this organization?" not "What do we now have available?" Remember the old story in which a man

67

encounters a boy looking around under a streetlamp. He asks "What are you looking for?" and the boy answers "The quarter I lost." The man asks "Where did you lose the quarter?" and the boy responds "There by the gutter." The man asks, incredulously, "Well why are you looking here by the lampost?" to which the boy replies "Because the light is so much better over here." Likewise, we must avoid the temptation of looking only where it is easy.

> *"One of the mistakes companies make is coming up with a list of what they could measure instead of what they should be measuring."*
> –Vicki Elliott

6) The Risk of Ratios. Beware the special risk involved anytime we use measures that are calculated as ratios. Return on Assets (ROA) and Defects per Million Opportunities (DPMO) are two common examples. As with most ratio measures, we use these two ratios because we want to track and improve the variable in the *numerator*. In ROA, that means improving our "return" or earnings; in DPMO, it means reducing our number of "defects." But, somewhere along the way, we determine that the measure would only be fair, valid, or comparable to others if we normalize it to some base. So we divide our "Return" by our "Assets" so we can make comparisons across large and small companies. And we divide "Defects" by "Million Opportunities" so we can make comparisons to other quality inspection situations. So far, so good.

What happens in actual practice? Well, people work hard to improve the numerator (Return or Defects) and often make quick gains. When the low-hanging fruit has been picked and gains become much harder, trouble sets in. People often start working on the denominator just to improve the ratio. In our examples above, managers begin to sell off corporate assets to reduce the ROA denominator, or quality analysts suddenly become better at counting additional millions of opportunities for defects to reduce the DPMO ratio. Their efforts are directed toward *managing the ratio*, not toward the original goal of improving organizational performance. Called "denominator management," this is a key risk we take on whenever we use a ratio measure. Watch for it.

7) Complex formulas. Difficult definitions and complicated formulas lead to distrust, especially if they apply to calculating bonuses, gainsharing or other rewards. Test the measurement definitions, calculations, and scorecard design on people from other groups; test them for easy comprehension. Try explaining them to people not involved in your work.

8) Drowning in metrics. An excessive number of metrics produces confusion from too many things to focus on. The sense of drowning in metrics is often traceable to measuring everything that can be measured, as is commonly done by the software used to manage call centers. And this confusion

69

can also come from poor measurement displays that do not use drilldowns, or from a hodgepodge of metrics that lack a framework to organize and communicate them. Careful thought and seeking the minimum number of indicators to track your critical success factors is the recommended approach.

Part 5

Doing the Work

- Starting Right
- Telling the Story

Starting Right

We have examined the leading concepts in metrics and the key tools for designing metrics. Now let's turn briefly to getting the job done in your organization.

Whatever your responsibility for metrics in your organization, you know that metrics design is not a one-person job. As you initiate a new metrics design or redesign, there are at least five things you'll want to consider to get started right: *leader, workgroup, advisor, plan,* and *predictive forecasting.*

1) **Leader.** While the work and accountability may be shared, someone in a leadership capacity must sponsor and direct the metrics effort. This person must make clear the results he or she wants.

2) **Workgroup.** Design your measures as a group effort. This practice always generates more good ideas, builds involvement and commitment, helps keep the design practical, and avoids mistakes by bringing out "what ifs" that are only known by those close to the action. How many should be in the design group? In most cases, three is the practical minimum and about eight is generally the maximum. Implementing metrics goes far beyond technical design; be sure your team includes people who understand organizational change and know how to get programs implemented.

3) **Advisor.** Determine whether you will want a third party, an internal or external consultant, to provide expertise and coaching. If you believe such a person would be helpful, get him or her involved early so your group gets off to a strong start and the effort does not stall. It is extremely valuable to have the members a workgroup involved in designing their own measures; they have crucial knowledge and must take ownership for the measures to be effective. If, however, the group lacks the specialized knowledge and experience required, you should get advisory help onboard well before difficulty arises, rather than after.

4) **Plan.** Even if you do not anticipate a large undertaking, it is wise to have a plan for your metrics work. A general plan will include results desired, timetable, key tasks, communications with the organization, deployment methods, and so forth. Perhaps most importantly, it will *anticipate the organizational change issues you will face*. Once the preliminary design is set, it's a good practice to get a key group together to devise *how* to make the program work—not to revisit the design but how to roll it out, how to communicate, and everything that must be done to make the implementation a success.

This is especially helpful if the group is too large to include everyone in the design effort.

5) **Predictive Forecasting.** After a set of metrics has been drafted, there is one special activity that can lead to new insights and important revisions before implementation. Predictive Forecasting works like organized brainstorming, in which a group of observers consider, metric by metric, what might happen after deployment. What will change? What new behaviors might people exhibit? What existing behaviors (good and bad) might change? What further consequences might result from these changes? This is one time when it helps to have "fresh eyes" and a cynical thinker or two in the group. If you practice this type of analysis, you are likely to be surprised by what it reveals and the new insights you gain. Those who omit this step are likely to have their surprises show up in real life. And they may be unpleasant.

Telling the Story

"An explanation should be as simple as possible, but no simpler." —Albert Einstein

Earlier, we noted that measurement frameworks have two valuable purposes. First they guide productive thinking as we define what performance means and the metrics that might best capture performance. Secondly, measurement frameworks serve a communicating role— they help structure and tell the story of our group's performance. Let us close our work on designing metrics by turning briefly to this communicating role.

Reporting performance. Some years ago, the president of a large bank showed us his monthly performance report. It was a bound volume of about 400 pages; on each page was a table with roughly 40 columns and 60 rows of numbers in tiny, eight-point type. The hundreds of thousands of numbers in this report represented the performance of the bank during the past month. We have all seen this type of output, where the report does not really inform anyone but, instead, becomes a reference document for looking up facts.

By contrast, the best practices in management reporting today follow certain principles:

1) Graphical. The best performance reports today, in paper and on the web, are increasingly graphical. Usually

75

showing trends over time, these graphs paint pictures of performance that communicate clearly and allow the reader's mind to immediately grasp key conclusions. In telling the story of performance, a picture is still worth a thousand words.

The methods and principles of visually presenting information have been extensively explored and illustrated in the work of Edward Tufte[4]. His many articles and books on this topic are highly recommended.

2) Focused. Rather than accumulating and presenting a mass of individual numbers, like the bank report noted earlier, the best management reports today tell the story of performance in terms of issues—critical success factors like customer service, cost of funding, manufacturing efficiency, customer retention, systems deployment, etc.

3) Structured. Here is where a metrics frameworks plays its communicating role. Though measures may illustrate performance on a number of Critical Success Factors, the best performance reports today are also structured to tell a coherent story—they follow an organizing framework that helps the reader to grasp what is important about this organization's performance. They will help show the issues that are being balanced. If you are using a Balanced Scorecard framework, the report structure will follow the

Financial, Customer, Processes, Learning/Growth pattern or some modification of it. Or, the report structure might follow the Effectiveness, Efficiency, and Strategic Change pattern of the Enterprise Performance Framework, or some other framework.

So, modern performance reports, assisted greatly by critical success factors and a measurement framework, are geared to telling the story of performance in a visual, coherent, compelling manner.

We offer our best wishes in your efforts to design the right metrics and to tell the performance story of your organization or workgroup.

References and Notes

[1]Johnson, H. T. and Kaplan, R. S. *Relevance Lost: The Rise and Fall of Management Accounting* (Boston: Harvard Business School Press, 1987).

[2]Kaplan, R. S. and Norton, D. P. "The Balanced Scorecard: Measures that Drive Performance," *Harvard Business Review* (Jan-Feb 1992).

[3]Kaplan, R. S. and Norton, D. P. *The Strategy Focused Organization* (Boston: Harvard Business School Publishing Corporation, 2001).

[4]Tufte, E. *The Visual Display of Quantitative Information* (Cheshire, Connecticut: Graphics Press, 1983). Also see the many other works by Tufte, including *Envisioning Information* and *Visual Explanations: Images, Quantities, Evidence and Narrative.*

Final notes. . .

Other books in this series include:
Measuring Performance (ISBN 0-9702471-1-7)
Crafting Strategy (ISBN 0-9702471-0-9)

As schedules permit, Dr. Frost is available to provide advisory services, telephone consultations, and speaking engagements on performance metrics and related topics.

More copies?

For quick service and volume discounts on our publications, call the publisher direct at 214-350-1082 or e-mail: books@MeasurementInternational.com

Number of copies required: _____

Name: _____

Title: _____

Company: _____

Address: _____

City, State, ZIP: _____

Phone:_____ E-mail:_____